W9-BMS-594

The World of Nature

SEASHELLS

GALLERY BOOKS
An Imprint of W. H. Smith Publishers Inc.
112 Madison Avenue
New York City 10016

The Image Bank® is a registered trademark of
The Image Bank, Inc.

Copyright © The Image Bank 1990. All rights reserved.
No part of this publication may be reproduced,
stored in a retrieval system, transmitted
or used in any form or by any means,
electronic, mechanical, photocopying, recording
or otherwise without the prior permission
of the copyright holder.

This edition first published in U.S.
in 1990 by Gallery Books,
an imprint of W.H. Smith Publishers, Inc.
112 Madison Avenue, New York, New York 10016

ISBN 0-8317-9578-6

Printed and bound in Spain

All photographs by James H. Carmichael, Jr.

For rights information about the photographs in
this book please contact:

The Image Bank
111 Fifth Avenue, New York, N.Y. 10003

Producer: Solomon M. Skolnick
Author: Harald A. Rehder, Ph.D.
Design Concept: Leslie Ehlers
Designer: Ann-Louise Lipman
Editor: Madelyn Larsen
Production: Valerie Zars
Photo Researcher: Edward Douglas
Assistant Photo Researcher: Robert Hale

Opposite: Hirase's Slit Shell is one of about 20 known living species of an ancient family once abundant 200 million years ago. (*Pleurotomaria hirasei* Pilsbry, 1903. 4 in./10 cm).

Abalones, or Sea Ears, are low-spired shells with a large, ear-shaped body whorl. The Canaliculate Abalone is a relatively small species with varied coloring. (*Haliotis parva* L., 1758. 1.5 in./4 cm). Below: In contrast, Emma's Abalone grows to more than twice the size of the Canaliculate. (*Haliotis emmae* Reeve, 1846. 4 in./10 cm).

The shells that are the subject of this book are the hard, calcareous, protective structures secreted by a mollusk, protecting its soft body from the environment and predators.

Mollusks comprise the phylum Mollusca among the invertebrate animals in the animal kingdom. After the insects the mollusks, with about 150,000 different kinds, are the second-largest group in the animal kingdom.

The molluscan animal is soft-bodied (the word *mollusk* is derived from the Greek adjective *malakos*, meaning "soft"). The body wall that surrounds the organs has a fleshy extension called the mantle, whose glands secrete the materials to

Top to bottom: Because they live in deep water, all Slit Shells are uncommon in collections. Moderately large and low-spired, Teramachi's Slit Shell is found off Japan. (*Pleurotomaria teramachii* Kuroda, 1955. 4.5 in./11.4 cm). One of the rarest is Victor Dan's Slit Shell from the Philippines. (*Pleurotomaria vicdani* Kosuge, 1980). The Lovely Slit Shell is also found in deep water. It lives off the coast of Florida. (*Pleurotomaria amabilis* Bayer, 1963. 3 in./7 cm).

form the shell. Mollusks possess gills, organs that can extract oxygen from the sea water as it passes over them, and usually one or two siphons, one for taking water and food and the other for expelling water and wastes.

The phylum Mollusca is divided into five main groups or classes (and several smaller classes that do not concern us here), of which four – the gastropods *(Gastropoda)*, the bivalves *(Bivalvia)*, the chitons *(Polyplacophora)* and the cephalopods *(Cephalopoda)* – are represented in this book. The fifth class, the tusk shells *(Scaphopoda)*, have elongated, tusk-like shells, are generally white, and live in shallow to deep water.

The animals of each class differ in the presence or absence of a foot and its form and position, and in the presence or absence of a head, as well as in

Top to bottom: Found grazing among the kelp beds on the California coast, the Ringed Top is probably the most beautiful of our American Top Shells. (*Calliostoma annulatum* (Lightfoot, 1786). 1 in./2.5 cm). The Superb Gaza has been dredged in some numbers in recent years, although it is still rare in collections. (*Gaza superba* (Dall, 1881). 1.2 in./3 cm). The common West Indian Top is mainly used as a food source. (*Cittarium pica* (L., 1758). 3 in./7 cm).

The Japanese Black-lined Limpet, like most Limpets, creeps slowly over rocks, grazing on minute plant and animal life. (*Cellana nigrolineata* (Reeve, 1854). 2 in./5cm). Below: The Great Keyhole Limpet from California is the largest living member of its family. (*Megathura crenulata* (Sowerby, 1825). 3 in./7.5 cm).

This page: The Silver-mouth Turban is one of the most common shells on Pacific tropic reefs. (*Turbo argyrostomus* L., 1758. 3 in./7 cm). Found along the southeastern coast of the U.S. and throughout the Caribbean, the common Chestnut Turban varies considerably in sculpture and color markings. (*Turbo castaneus* Gmelin, 1791). 1.5 in./3.5 cm). Opposite: Many beautiful shells are found in the Phillipines. One of the most colorful species of its genus is Kiener's Delphinula. (*Angaria sphaerula* (Kiener, 1839). 2 in./5 cm). The rare and beautiful Girgyllus Bolma is a deep-water shell. (*Bolma girgyllus* (Reeve, 1861). 2 in./5 cm). Victor Dan's Delphinula, is a rare shell with delicate spiny sculpture. (*Angaria vicdani* (Kosuge, 1980). 2 in./5 cm). Overleaf: This highly variable shell, the Zigzag Nerite, lives in vast numbers on mudflats in brackish water estuaries. (*Neritina communis* Quoy & Gaimard, 1832). 0.5 in./1.2 cm).

other details. Similarly the shells of these classes differ greatly, as we will see.

The shell of the gastropods is formed essentially of one piece that is generally spirally and regularly twisted about a central axis. Sometimes the spiral aspect of the shell is lost and the shell becomes conical, plate-shaped or cap-shaped. The gastropod animal typically has a relatively large foot on which it progresses, and a well-defined head with paired eyes and tentacles, or "feelers."

The bivalve shell, on the other hand, consists of two, more or less equal and symmetrical pieces, hinged at the top by a horny ligament. The animal of the bivalve has no head, eyes or tentacles and can be completely within the shell. Its organs are surrounded by a pair of fleshy lobes that have glands that secrete material to form the paired valves. Basically there is a muscular wedge-shaped foot of varying size and form that the bivalve uses to move through the sand or mud. The foot becomes lost in those bivalves, like the oyster or jingle shell, which adhere to hard surfaces.

The chitons are mollusks with a flattened, symmetrical, oval or elongated body, with a broad foot, a head that lacks eyes or tentacles, and a series of

Opposite: Found in southern Australia, the Australian Pheasant has a smooth shell with an extremely variable color pattern. (*Phasianella australis* (Gmelin, 1791). 2.5 in./6 cm). The attractive little Zebra Nerite, with its orange mouth and black stripes, is abundant in tidepools in the Florida Keys and West Indies. (*Puperita pupa* (L., 1758). 0.7 in./1.8 cm). This page: The tiny, gemlike Pacific Emerald Nerite is common locally, found in shallow water on marine grasses. (*Smaragdia ngiana* (Recluz, 1841). 0.3 in./7 mm). A member of a group of Winkles that often lives on rocks above the high-tide line, the Coronate Prickly Winkle is found in the Philippines. (*Tectarius coronatus* (Valenciennes, 1832). 1.5 in./3.5 cm).

This page: The Clear Sundial is a handsome, low-spired shell, common in some localities of the Indo-Pacific region. (*Architectonica perspectiva* (L., 1758). 2 in./5 cm). Once considered a rare and valuable shell, the Precious Wentletrap is now found in many collections. (*Epitonium scalare* (L., 1758). 2 in./5 cm. Opposite: When the Precious Wentletrap commanded a high price, skilled Chinese workers made forged specimens out of rice paste. (*Epitonium scalare* (L., 1758)).

gills on each side between the mantle and the foot. The shell consists of eight shelly, overlapping plates. The shell is surrounded by a muscular flexible girdle that holds the plates together, which allows the animal, when disturbed, to roll up like a pill-bug.

Finally the cephalopods *(Cephalopeda)* constitute a class that includes the octopus, squid and cuttlefish. They possess a head with well-developed eyes and nervous system and eight arms furnished with suckers, surrounding a mouth with a strong, horny beak resembling that of a parrot. One large group has two long tentacles in addition to the eight arms. The members of the Nautilus family are the only ones with a completely external shell.

Top to bottom: A relatively uncommon shell, the Rooster-tail Conch is an inhabitant of shallow water in the Caribbean. (*Strombus gallus* (L., 1758). 4.5 in./11.5 cm). Also uncommon is Lister's Conch, found in both the Bay of Bengal and the Indian Ocean. (*Strombus listeri* (Gray, 1852). 5 in./13 cm). The Orange Spider Conch, like other Spider Conchs, feeds on algae and is found in the Indian and western Pacific Oceans. (*Lambis crocata* (Link, 1807). 4.5 in./11.5 cm).

Parts of the Shell

The gastropod shell consists basically of a shelly tube that is wound spirally on a central axis, similar to a spiral staircase. As the shell grows, the turns or whorls of the shell become increasingly larger, and the final turn is called the body whorl, which ends in an opening known as the aperture. In some groups the animal can withdraw completely into the shell and close itself in with a shelly or horny door, or *operculum*. The part of the shell above the aperture is the spire, and the aperture may be drawn out below into an open canal or a more or less closed tube of varying length called the anterior canal.

In some shells the body whorl may increase greatly in size and make up most of the shell, as in the Abalones. In the limpets and in some other groups, the earliest spiral

Top to bottom: One of the larger members of the Cowrie Family, the Eyed Cowrie is found on coral reefs in the Indo- Pacific region. (*Cypraea argus* L., 1758. 3 in./7.5 cm). Most members of the group to which the Banded Bonnet belongs feed on sand dollars and sea urchins. (*Phalium bandatum* (Perry, 1811). 3.5 in./9 cm). A distinctive member of the Cowrie Family, Jenner's Cowrie is found on or near stony corals on the West Coast of Mexico and Central America (*Jenneria pustulata* (Lightfoot, 1786). 1 in./2.5 cm).

A member of the large Triton Family, the Atlantic Hairy Triton is found from southern Florida to northern Brazil. (*Cymatium martinianum* (d'Orbigny, 1846). 3 in./7.5 cm). Below: The Uncommon Pearl Triton, found in the Indo-Pacific region, is carnivorous. (*Cymatium pyrum* (L., 1758).3 in./7.5 cm).

The small, flattened and knobby shell of the Tadpole Triton is found in the tropical western Pacific. (*Gyrineum gyrinum* (L., 1758). 1 in./2.5 cm). Below: Pacific Islanders have long knocked the tip off of the Trumpet Triton and used it to call the people together for ceremonial purposes. (*Charonia tritonis* (L., 1758).13 in./33 cm).

whorls are few and are soon lost by being broken or worn off, leaving only a conical or plate-shaped body whorl. Some gastropods are broad, with a low conical spire; others may be elongated, with a high spire and many whorls, like the Augers. Families with a small spire, large body whorl and narrow aperture are the Olives and the Cones. In the Cowry family the body whorl extends over and covers the small spire in the final stage of its growth, and the aperture becomes very narrow. The aperture may be furnished with teeth or strong folds on either or both sides. The body whorl and spire may be smooth or ornamented with axial ribs (*lamellae*), axially aligned rows of spines or fronds, or spiral ridges.

Top to bottom: The fronds of the Pendant Murex are often tinged with a delicate pink. (*Chicoreus aculeatus* (Lamarck, 1822). 2 in./5 cm). The Maurus Murex, a stout, dark shell with pink fronds, appears to be found only in the Marquesas Islands of Polynesia. (*Chicoreus maurus* (Broderip, 1833). 3 in./7.5 cm). The Venus Comb Murex is found in the western Pacific Ocean. (*Murex pecten* Lightfoot, 1786). 4 in./ 10 cm).

All the bivalves illustrated in this book have valves that externally are approximately mirror-images of each other. These valves are held together not only by one or more muscles, the scars of which are often plainly visible where they are attached to the valves, but also generally by a horny ligament attached to both valves at the upper margin or hinge line. A series of few to many interlocking teeth may be present at the upper margin to keep the valves properly aligned. As the photographs show, the ornamentation and color patterns exhibit a great range of variability. The exterior surface may be smooth or sculptured by axial ribs or concentric ridges, or a combination of both. These ribs may be spiny or lamellar with plate-like ridges.

The eight plates or valves of the chitons may be almost flat or strongly arched, occasionally with an angled ridge running down the center of the shell. The valves may vary from smooth to strongly structured. The girdle may surround the valves as a narrow belt, or it may be wide, partly intruding between the valves; occasionally it covers most of the valves, leaving only the central part of each valve exposed. In one large species from California and Alaska the girdle, which is reddish and grainy, actually completely covers the valves. The girdle may be smooth and leathery or densely covered

This is an unusual color form of the large and common Ramose Murex, usually white with obscure, brown lines and an aperture tinged with pink. (*Chicoreus ramosus* (L., 1758). 8 in./20 cm). Below: Members of the Murex Family are carnivorous, feeding on mollusks and other invertebrates. Saul's Murex is from the southwestern Pacific. (*Chicoreus saulii* (Sowerby, 1841). 4 in./10 cm).

The Frilled Dogwinkle is among the most common and variable gastropods found on the rocks of the coast from California to Alaska. (*Nucella lamellosa* (Gmelin, 1791). 2.5 in./6 cm). Below: A member of the group of tropical Whelks, the Areola Babylonia is found in sand off the coast of southeast Asia. (*Babylonia areolata* (Link, 1807).2.5 in./6.5 cm).

with shelly scales, beads or spicules; it may also be furnished with tufts of bristles near the spaces between the valves.

The cephalopods are represented in this book by one species, the Common Chambered Nautilus, a species that as it grows in size seals off the back part of the old chamber and moves forward into the new, larger chamber.

Man's Use of Shells

Although in this book we are dealing with the shells of mollusks, it should be noted that the animals of many species of mollusks have been for man since time immemorial an important source of food. So before we discuss the role that shells played, and still do play, in the cultural and social activities of man we should say a few words about how man has used the soft fleshy animals that make and inhabit these shells.

Top to bottom: One of the largest of Californian gastropods, the Giant Forreria is frequently found near oyster beds, where it feeds. (*Forreria belcheri* (Hinds, 1843).5 in./13 cm). The Wide-spined Latiaxis is an uncommon, umbilicate shell. (*Latiaxis latipinnatus* Azuma, 1961. 1 in./2.5 cm). A member of the Dove-Shell Family, the Elegant Strombina belongs to a genus restricted to tropical American waters. *Strombina elegans* (Sowerby, 1832). 1.3 in./3.5 cm).

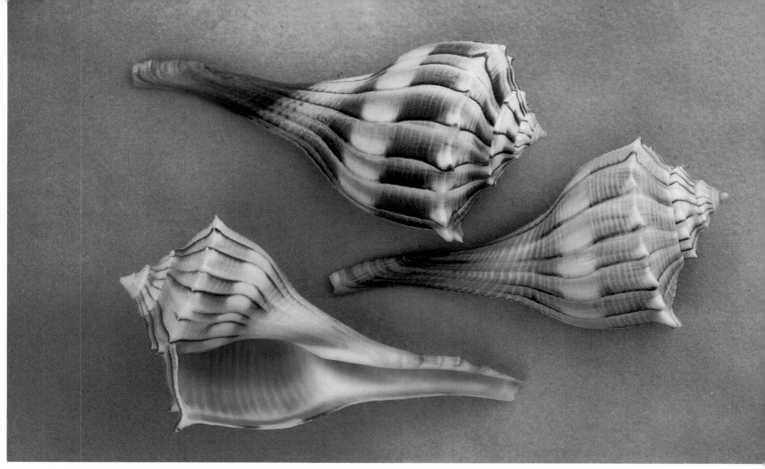

Opposite: The Tabled Neptune, one of a largely coldwater group of Neptune Whelks, is found in deep water off California and western Canada. (*Neptunea tabulata* (Baird, 1863). 3 in./7.5 cm). This page: Named for its interrupted axial lines on the body whorl, the left-handed, or sinistral, Lightning Whelk is commonly found on the southeastern coast of the U.S. (*Busycon contrarium* (Conard, 1840). to 16 in./40 cm). Below: Related to the Lightning Whelk, the uncommon Turnip Whelk is found in moderate depths in the western Gulf of Mexico. (*Busycon coarctatum* (Sowerby, 1825). 5 in./13 cm).

A member of the Spindle-Shell Family, the Indo-Pacific Fleshy Peristernia is noted for the dark interspaces between the yellowish ribs and the purplish aperture. (*Peristernia incarnata* (Kiener, 1840). 1 in./2.5 cm). Below: The Florida Horse Conch is the largest gastropod shell in America, and one of the two largest in the world. (*Pleuroploca gigantea* (Kiener, 1840). to 2 ft./60 cm). Opposite: A relatively common shell on the west coast of Mexico and Central America, the Thorn Latirus probably uses its long spine to open shellfish. (*Opeatostoma pseudodon* (Burrow, 1815). 1.5 in./4 cm).

The rather rare, strikingly colored Red-lipped Olive is found in the New Hebrides and New Caledonia. (*Oliva rubrolabiata* H. Fischer, 1902). 1.7 in./4.5 cm). Below: The Tent Olive is the largest member of this family of carnivorous mollusks. It is found from the Gulf of California to Panama. (*Oliva orphyria* L., 1758). 3.5 in./ 9 cm).

Because mollusks are found in abundance along the shores of the oceans, bays, in rivers and lakes, early man quickly learned to gather them in numbers, crack them open and eat the fleshy animals. The mounds of the shells of oysters, clams and mussels that are found along parts of the coast of North America attest to this fact. Kitchen middens, as these heaps of shells are called, discarded after feasting on mollusks for decades if not hundreds of years, are also found in many parts of the world.

At the present time the commercial cultivation and gathering of mollusks, especially oysters, clams and mussels, is carried on throughout the world. The science of farming our edible marine resources – mariculture or aquiculture – is widespread and we can expect to see an increase in this practice as regards mollusks, for there are many species not now

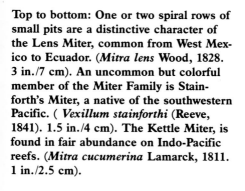

Top to bottom: One or two spiral rows of small pits are a distinctive character of the Lens Miter, common from West Mexico to Ecuador. (*Mitra lens* Wood, 1828. 3 in./7 cm). An uncommon but colorful member of the Miter Family is Stainforth's Miter, a native of the southwestern Pacific. (*Vexillum stainforthi* (Reeve, 1841). 1.5 in./4 cm). The Kettle Miter, is found in fair abundance on Indo-Pacific reefs. (*Mitra cucumerina* Lamarck, 1811. 1 in./2.5 cm).

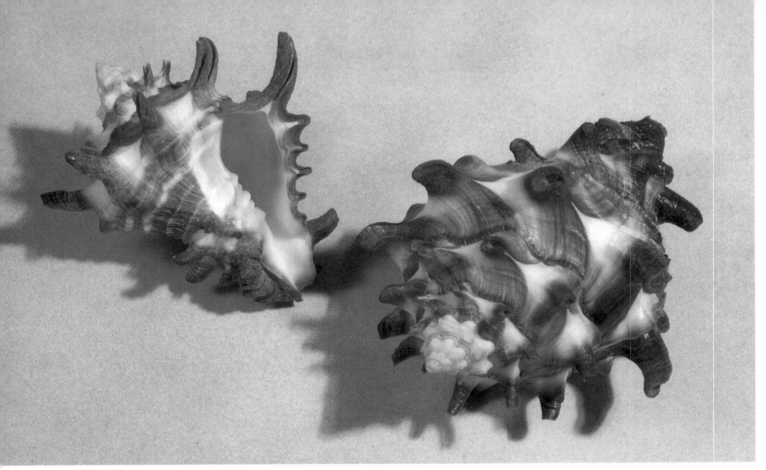

The Imperial Vase, found only in a relatively small area in the central Philippines, is rare in collections. (*Vasum tubiferum* (Anton, 1839). 3 in./7.5 cm). Below: A relatively uncommon species that lives in moderate depths, the Spiny Caribbean Vase is found in the southern Caribbean. (*Vasum capitellum* (L., 1758). 2.5 in./6 cm). Opposite: The Helmet Vase – rather rare – has, in maturity, a flaring and crenulated outer lip that is molted purplish brown. (*Vasum cassiforme* (Kiener, 1841) 2.7 in./6.8 cm).

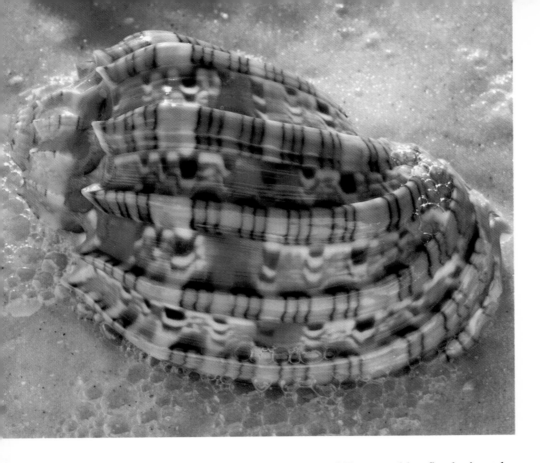

The True Harp is found from East Africa to Samoa and Tonga, and has fine horizontal lines on the axial ribs. (*Harpa harpa* (L., 1758). 2.8 in./7 cm). Below: The rare Imperial Harp is found mainly near Mauritius. Like other Harps, it feeds on crabs. (*Harpa costata* (L., 1758). 3.5 in./9 cm).

One other use of mollusks by ancient man and primitive peoples should be mentioned. In very early historic times the peoples living along the eastern edge of the Mediterranean discovered that the animals of certain species of the Murex Family when crushed and boiled could stain cloth a deep purple. The ancient Phoenicians took over this industry and made it into a rewarding monopoly. The dye was used for the robes of eastern rulers and for the togas of Roman senators. The Indians of Central America independently discovered that some species of the Rock Shell Family (Thaididae) yield a very similar dye for their textiles.

The most interesting use to which man has put shells is to ornament himself and his surroundings. Early European explorers to the United States found the Indians wearing shell ornaments on their clothing. On the East Coast beads made from the shell of the Quahog (*Mercenaria mercenaria* Linnaeus, 1758) of the Venus Clam Family were sewn on the deerskin clothing and also strung together and used as money. On the West Coast some tribes ornamented their clothing with rows of tusk shells, which were also used as money. Many species of the small, colorful used for food, especially in tropical waters, that could become important additions to our food resources.

Rare and colorful, Clover's Lyria is found only along a small area of southern Sri Lanka. (*Lyria cloveriana* Weaver, 1963. 3.2 in./ 8 cm). Below: The Heavy Baler (or Umbilicate Volute) is found in North Australia and New Guinea, and is used by the Aborigines to bail out their canoes. (*Melo umbilicatus* Sowerby, 1826. 12 in./30 cm)

Overleaf: Pictured here are various forms of the Common Music Volute of the Caribbean. The four short knobby specimens represent a form found in certain islands. Due to sexual dimorphism and variability, it is difficult to separate them into subspecies. (*Voluta musica* L., 1758. 3 in./8 cm). This page: An uncommon and beautiful species, the Lyre-formed Lyria is found in waters off East Africa. (*Lyria lyraeformis* (Swainson, 1821). 4 in./10 cm). Below: The upper figure is a dark form of Lyria lyraeformis (see above). The lower left specimen is Kuroda's Lyria from Taiwan (*Lyria kurodai* Kawamura, 1964). In the lower right is Delessert's Lyria from the western Indian Ocean (*Lyria delessertiana* (Petit, 1842). Opposite: A perfect Junonia is a treasure that all shell collectors of western Florida continually hope to find. (*Scaphella junonia* (Lamarck, 1804). 4 in./10 cm). Below: Eagerly sought-after by collectors is the Festive Lyria. (*Festilyria festiva* (Lamarck, 1811). 3 in./7.5 cm).

shells found on tropical beaches were strung together by local Indians and made into necklaces. In some of the Mayan ruins in Central America carved representations of some of the larger seashells may be seen on temple friezes.

In the Pacific Islands and in Africa people commonly decorate their houses and canoes with shells, especially various species of the Cowry Family. They wear headbands made from shells, and armbands, cut from certain shells like members of the Cone Family, are common. Early explorers encountered chiefs in Fiji who wore large, polished valves of the Pearl Oyster as neck pendants. In the past Pacific islanders also used shells in a variety of ways in their daily life: as canoe balers, cooking vessels and water containers. Certain large shells were cut so that they could be used to grind up coconut meat or scrape breadfruit. Many of these kinds of household objects are still used today.

At the present time, however, we make greatest use of shells and shell material in jewelry, decorative ornaments and such mundane clothing accessories as buttons. Especially popular for these uses are pearls and mother-of-pearl. The principal source of both is one of the two large species of

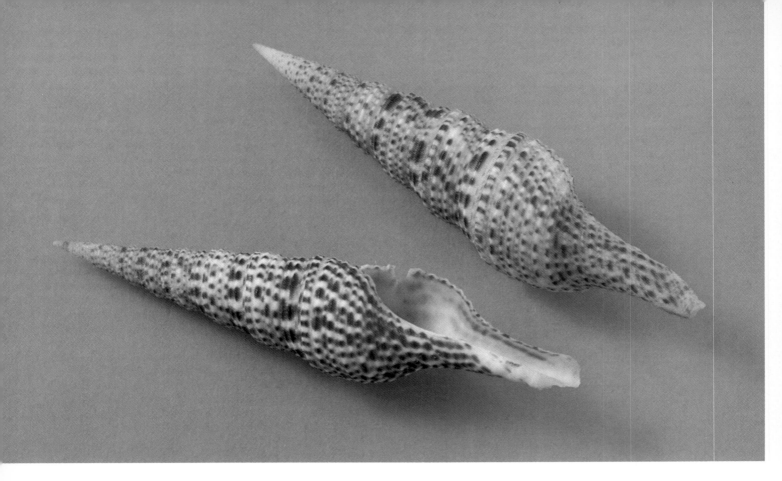

An uncommon species of a large, worldwide family, the Supreme Turrid is found in moderately deep water in the western Pacific and Indian Oceans. (*Turris crispa* (Lamarck, 1816). 6 in./15 cm). Below: This relatively common West African Cancellate Nutmeg shows the strong folds characteristic of the family. (*Cancellaria cancellata* (L., 1767). 1.2 in./3 cm).

The Matchless Cone is one of the more uncommon species of the genus. (*Conus cedonulli* (L., 1767). 2 in./5 cm). Below, from left to right: Rare or uncommon are Rhododendron Cone from the central Pacific (*Conus adamsonii* Broderip, 1836); Marquesas Cone from the Marquesas (*Conus marchionatus* Hinds, 1843); Gauguin's Cone from the Marquesas (*Conus gauguini* Richard & Salvat, 1974).

Pearl Oysters, the Black-lipped Pearl Oyster (*Pinctada margaritifera* Linnaeus, 1758). Although pearls are still obtained in many parts of the tropics by diving for the pearl oysters and examining them for the presence of pearls, in Japan and other areas success has been had in "farming" pearl oysters. The process involves inserting a small nucleus of shelly or plastic material in the young, living oyster. The oyster then is allowed to grow in submerged cages until it is of the proper size to harvest the pearl, which was created by repeated layers of pearly nacre covering the inserted nucleus.

The valves of the Pearl Oyster itself are polished and the surface carved with designs in relief, or it is cut to fashion such items such as earrings, broaches, lapel pins, and pendants.

Opposite: The many variatioins of the Pacific Cone's color and size makes it a collector's favorite. This page, top to bottom: The Matchless Cone is known only in the West Indies. (*Conus cedonulli*, (L., 1767). 2 in./5 cm). Once sought after, the Glory-of-the-Sea Cone is obtained more frequently and is no longer quite as rare. (*Conus gloriamaris* Chemnitz, 1777. 4 in./10 cm). Although it is almost as beautiful as the Glory-of-the-Sea when fresh, the Textile Cone is a common Cone of the Indo-Pacific. (*Conus textile* L., 1758. 3 in./7.5 cm).

A gastropod, the Troca Shell (*Trochus niloticus* Linnaeus, 1758), a member of the Top Shell Family *(Trochidae)* is a large, stout, conical, pearly shell, native to the Indian and western Pacific Oceans. It has recently been introduced into French Polynesia, where it is thriving. When polished it is cut into buttons, and also into table and mantle ornaments.

In the markets and along the sidewalks and at the airports of beach resorts all over the world, as well as in the towns that tourists visit, such as Papeete, Tahiti, Apia in Western Samoa, and Suva, Fiji, you will find vendors selling not only shell ornaments and the shells themselves but also necklaces made of small shells, often very artistically designed and intricately fashioned.

Top to bottom: Species of the rather variable Admiral Cone appear in both the Indian and western Pacific Oceans. (*Conus ammiralis* L., 1758. 2.5 in./6 cm). The Nussatela Cone is rather common to the Indo-Pacific. (*Conus nussatella* L., 1758. 1.2 in./3 cm). The Marbled Cone, like the Textile Cone, feeds on other mollusks; its poisonous barb has been implicated in some human fatalities. (*Conus marmoreus* L.,1758. 4 in./10 cm).

The Flame Auger is an uncommon species found in offshore waters from Texas to Brazil. (*Terebra taurina* Lightfoot, 1786. 4.3 in./11 cm). Right: The distinctively marked Ornate Auger occurs from the Gulf of California to the Galápagos. The Augers, like their allies the Turrids and Cones, are carnivorous, feeding mainly on marine worms. (*Terebra ornata* Gray, 1834. 3.3 in./8.5 cm).

When the traveler arrives at the airport in Tahiti he or she is greeted with fragrant flower lei. On leaving the island, however, relatives, friends and acquaintances purchase shell necklaces to hang around the neck of the departing traveler. Of course, the longer you have been in the islands, and the more friends you have, the greater number of necklaces you receive. It becomes a mark of your popularity and a sort of a status symbol. Some travelers are so weighed down by necklaces that the lower part of their faces are almost covered.

Collecting and Studying Shells

Shells, or mollusks, are without doubt the most widely collected objects in the whole animal kingdom. With good reason. Shells frequently are very colorful and have interesting forms and intricate sculpture and many can be found on beaches, sandflats or rocky shores, often in good condition and needing little cleaning or preparation before placing them in a collection.

Opposite: The animal of the thin-shelled Brown-lined Paper Bubble has folds that cover most of the delicate shell when alive. (*Hydatina vesicaria* (Lightfoot, 1786). 2 in./5 cm). The Lined Bubble is widespread in the Indo-Pacific region, but is not common, though its attractively colored shell makes it readily recognizable. (*Bullina lineata* (Gray, 1825). 1 in./ 2.5 cm).

Found in the Florida Keys and West Indies, the West Indian Chiton has sculptured valves as well as a girdle that is paved with scales. (*Chiton tubercalatus* L., 1758. 2.5 in./6 cm). Below: Common on rocks and in tidepools of the Florida Keys and West Indies, the Rough-girdled Chiton often has eroded valves and a girdle with cluster of flattened bristles. (*Ceratozona squalida* (C.B. Adams, 1845). 1.5 in./4 cm). Overleaf: Brightly colored and variable, the Royal Cloak Scallop is abundant throughout the tropical Pacific. (*Gloripallium pallium* (L., 1758). 2 in./5 cm).

A yellowish form is unusual for the Lion's Paw, a shell that is found from North Carolina to Brazil. (*Nodipecten nodosus* (L., 1758). 4.4 in./11cm). Below: Discovered off the coast of Somalia, this colorful new species, Cranmers' Scallop, has been only recently described. (*Somalipecten cranmerorum* Waller, 1986. 2.5 in./6 cm).

An uncommon species, the Blood-stained Scallop is found only in the Red Sea and adjacent parts of the Indian Ocean. (Excellichlamys maculosus (Forsskal, 1775). 1 in./2.5 cm). Below: The Magnificent Scallop is a large species that is found in the Galápagos and the nearby coast of Ecuador. (*Lyropecten magnificus* (Sowerby, 1835). 7 in./17.5 cm).

Shells have been collected as objects of interest since ancient times. In the ruins of Pompeii, destroyed in A.D. 79 by an eruption of Vesuvius, a considerable collection of shells was found that may have belonged to the naturalist Pliny the Elder or to one of his scholars.

The St. James Scallop gets its name from the fact that pilgrims who had visited the shrine of St. James of Compostela in Spain affixed its shell to their hat or cloak. (*Pecten jacobaeus* L., 1758). 5 in./12 cm). Below: The Lion's Paw can reach a size of six inches, and is a favorite of collectors. (*Nodipecten nodosus* (L., 1758). 6 in./15 cm).

During the Renaissance many wealthy noblemen and merchants formed collections or "cabinets of natural curiosities," and illustrated books describing these collections were published in the seventeenth and eighteenth centuries. By the nineteenth century the collecting had become

The smaller and more intricate Splendid Scallop is related to the Royal Cloak Scallop. (*Gloripallium speciosum* (Reeve, 1853). 1.5 in./4 cm). Below: A rather large, thick shell, the Australian Cardita is moderately common in eastern Australia and the West Pacific. (*Cardita crassicosta* Lamarck, 1819. 3 in./7.5 cm)

much more sophisticated, due partly to the vast amount of new species coming in from the many voyages of exploration. Also, specialists published illustrated volumes of descriptions of shells, shops sprang up where shells were bought and sold, and auction houses from time to time auctioned off large collections. Several scientific journals dealing only with mollusks were started up in the 1840's and 1850's.

Specimens of the Thorny Oyster, especially those in quiet waters, can develop long and delicate spines. (*Spondylus americanus* Hermann, 1781. 4 in./10 cm). Below: The Victor Cockle is found in deep water in the West Pacific. (*Ctenocardium victor* (Angas, 1872). 1 in./2.5 cm). Opposite: The Oxheart Clam lives in ancient seas and is found from Norway to the Mediterranean. (*Glossus humanus* (L., 1758). 3.5 in./9 cm).

At the present time the collecting and study of mollusks is at an all-time high the world over. In the United States alone, there are about 35 local clubs or societies devoted to the furtherance of the study and collection of mollusks, with both professionals and amateurs as members. Many of them hold annual shell shows at which members and visitors compete for prizes. Many shell dealers attend these shows as well. These two national organizations hold annual meetings: the American Malacological Union (Constance E. Boone, Recording Secretary, 3706 Rice Boulevard, Houston, TX 77005), and the Conchologists of America

Preceding page: Heart Cockles (the genus *Corculum* comprises several species and varieties. (1.5 in./4 cm). This page: A common Mediterranean shell, the Hians Cockle is noted for its gaping shell and spines at both ends. (*Ringicardium hians* (Brocchi, 1814). 3 in./7.5 cm). The Thick-ribbed Cardita is found from the Gulf of California to Peru. (*Cardites crassicostata* (Sowerby, 1825). 2 in./5 cm). The Oxheart Clam, is used as a food source in parts of Europe. (*Glossus humanus.* (L., 1758). 3.5 in./9 cm). Below: The Hieroglyphic Venus at upper left. (*Lioconcha hieroglyphica* (Conrad, 1837), and the Camp Pitar Venus at lower right (*Lioconcha castrensis* (L., 1758), are both from the Indo-Pacific region.

(Walter E. Sage, Department of Invertebrates, American Museum of Natural History, New York, NY 10024). (The terms *conchology* and *malacology* are often used interchangeably, but the distinction is that the former denotes the study or knowledge of shells and the latter the study of the whole organism, the shell and the animal that makes the shell.)

There are also shell clubs in countries all over the world, many of which, like those in the United States, publish newsletters and journals. In the pages of these publications you can find everything from the names of members who wish to exchange shells and dealers' advertisements to ads for guided field trips to exotic places.

Opposite: Venus Clams can belong to various genera and species. This page, top to bottom: The thick-ribbed Imperial Venus is found from Cape Hatteras to Brazil. (*Chione latilirata* (Conrad, 1841). 1 in./2.5 cm). Common in the Indo-Pacific are the Textile Venus (*Paphia textile* (Gmelin, 1791). 3 in./7.5 cm) at top, and the Lettered Venus (*Tapes literatus* (L., 1758). 3.5 in./9 cm) at the bottom. Common to shallow waters in South Australia is the Wedding Cake Venus. (*Callanaitis disjecta* (Perry, 1811). 1.5 in./6 cm).

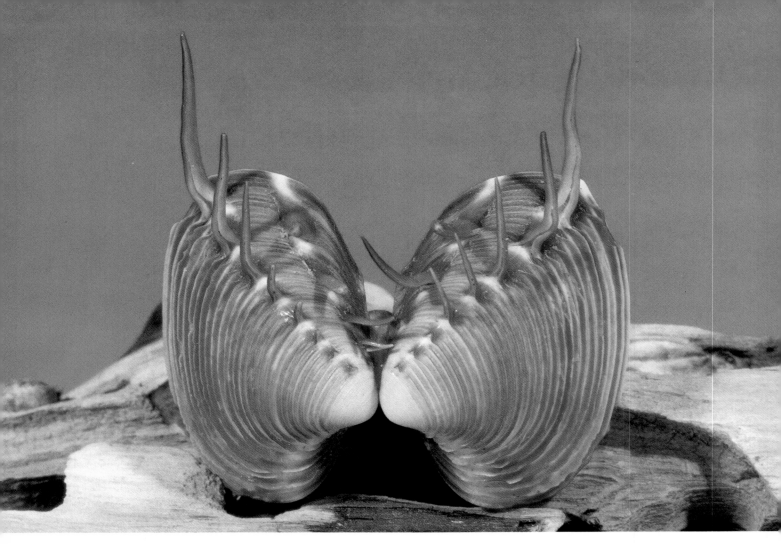

A dark form of the usually white Prostitute Venus, which can be found from West Mexico to Peru. (*Pitar lupanaria* (Lesson, 1830). 2 in./5 cm). Below: The long spines of the Prostitute Venus may help to anchor the shell in shifting surface sands. (*Pitar lupanaria* (Lesson, 1830).

The Angel Wing is found in muddy sandflats on the west coast of Florida; an internal pink band is a rare feature. (*Cyrtopleura costata* (L., 1758). 6 in./15 cm). Below: A colorful specimen of a Dosinia Clam from the Pacific whose identity is still unknown. (*Dosinia species*).

Preceding page: Specimens of the Common Chambered Nautilus, the sectioned one showing the chambers, successfully sealed off as the Nautilus grows. (*Nautilus pompilius* L., 1758. 6 in./15 cm).

DEP.LEG. B-44.675-89